Love for All Seasons

Love For All Seasons

SELECTED BY Kitty Clevenger

ILLUSTRATED BY Fred Klemushin

CALLIGRAPHY BY Rick Cusick

♛ HALLMARK CROWN EDITIONS

LOVE FOR ALL SEASONS

As soft and gentle
as a summer breeze...
as radiant and beautiful
as autumn
in all its finery...
as warm and friendly
as a cozy fire
on a frosty winter night...
as refreshing and delightful
as the springtime flowers...
you are my love for all seasons!

LOVE SONG

Sweep the house clean,

hang fresh curtains

in the windows

put on a new dress

and come with me!

The elm is scattering

its little loaves

of sweet smells

from a white sky!

Who shall hear of us
in the time to come?
Let him say there was
a burst of fragrance
from black branches.

WILLIAM CARLOS WILLIAMS

TO A GOLDEN-HAIRED GIRL IN A LOUISIANA TOWN

You are a sunrise,
If a star should rise instead of the sun.
You are a moonrise,
If a star should come in the place of the moon.
You are the Spring,
If a face should bloom instead of an apple-bough.
You are my love,
If your heart is as kind
As your young eyes now.

VACHEL
LINDSAY

INTOXICATION

Neath a willow with ivy entangled
We take cover in blustery weather.
My arms are wreathed about you;
In my raincape we huddle together.

I was wrong: Not ivy, my dearest,
But hops encircle this willow.
Well, then, let's spread in its shelter
My cape for a rug and a pillow!

Boris Pasternak

DEW

AS DEW LEAVES THE COBWEB LIGHTLY
  THREADED WITH STARS,
SCATTERING JEWELS ON THE FENCE
  AND THE PASTURE BARS;
AS DAWN LEAVES THE DRY GRASS BRIGHT
  AND THE TANGLED WEEDS
BEARING A RAINBOW GEM
  ON EACH OF THEIR SEEDS;
SO HAS YOUR LOVE, MY LOVER,
  FRESH AS THE DAWN,
MADE ME A SHINING ROAD
  TO TRAVEL ON,
SET EVERY COMMON SIGHT
  OF TREE OR STONE
DELICATELY ALIGHT
  FOR ME ALONE

Sara Teasdale

AFTER TWO YEARS

She is all so slight
And tender and white
As a May morning.
She walks without hood
At dusk.   It is good
To hear her sing.

It is God's will
That I shall love her still
As He loves Mary,
And night and day
I will go forth to pray
That she love me.

RICHARD ALDINGTON

July Midnight

FIREFLIES FLICKER IN THE TOPS OF TREES,
FLICKER IN THE LOWER BRANCHES,
SKIM ALONG THE GROUND.
OVER THE MOON-WHITE LILIES
IS A FLASHING AND CEASING OF SMALL,
      LEMON-GREEN STARS.
AS YOU LEAN AGAINST ME,
MOON-WHITE,
THE AIR ALL ABOUT YOU
IS SLIT, AND PRICKED, AND POINTED
   WITH SPARKLES OF LEMON-GREEN FLAM
STARTING OUT OF A BACKGROUND
      OF VAGUE, BLUE TREES.

Amy Lowell

Rain

I have always hated the rain,

And the gloom of grayed skies.

But now I think I must always cherish

Rain-hung leaf and the misty river;

And the friendly screen of dripping green

Where eager kisses were shyly given

And your pipe-smoke made clouds

    in our damp, close heaven.

The curious laggard passed us by,
His wet shoes soughed on the shining walk.
And that afternoon was filled

with a blurred glory —
that afternoon, when we first talked
as lovers.

JEAN STARR UNTERMEYER

IT'S ALL I HAVE
TO BRING TODAY

It's all I have to bring today,

This, and my heart beside,

This, and my heart, and all the fields,

And all the meadows wide.

Be sure you count, should I forget—

Some one the sum could tell—

This, and my heart, and all the bees

Which in the clover dwell.

EMILY DICKINSON

MY LOVE
COMES WALKING

My love comes walking,
And these flowers
That never saw her til this day
Look up; but then
Bend down straightway.

My love sees nothing here but me,
Who never trembled thus before;
And glances down
Lest I do more.

My love is laughing.
Those wild things
Were never tame until I too,
Down-dropping, kissed
Her silvery shoe.

(MARK VAN DOREN

BUTTERCUP FIELDS

I remember our first summer...

Buttercup fields

And the scent of hay,

I remember evening falling...

And walking hand in hand

At the close of day.

Sunsets seemed so much more lovely...

Than sunsets

Ever seemed before,

When you and I would walk together...

In buttercup fields

In the days of yore.

Somehow summer never left us...
We saved its sunshine
In our hearts
And never knew the chill of winter...
For we shared the warmth
That love imparts
Thanks for all the joys of summer...
More than that,
What can I say?
Except that always I'll remember...
Buttercup fields
And the scent of hay.

ROB WOOD

Afterwards

AFTERWARDS
 IT IS NOT THE KISS WE REMEMBER—
ONLY THAT ONE DAY IN GOLD SEPTEMBER
YOUR SPIRIT MET MY SPIRIT,
 AND WE CLUNG
TOGETHER—WORDLESS FOR ONE MOMENT, HUNG
IN SPACE.... AFTERWARDS RECALLING—
 NOT THE GREETING,
AND NOT THE KISS...
 BUT JUST OUR SPIRITS MEETING!

Anne Campbell

Treasured Memory

As days grow short, I keep remembering
One day in autumn, long ago,
When certain doubts and cares had been resolved,
And you, long absent, in a glow
Of happiness, were home. In glorious woods
We walked loved paths, in air as sweet
As were our thoughts; sometimes a late bird san
And bright leaves whispered at our feet.

We knew then without doubt, that Heaven is,
That with deep love and perfect weather
It can touch earth. It filled our hearts,
As we strolled autumn woods together.

Clara Aiken Speer

OCTOBER FIRES

Red flames and yellow flames
Are burning up the residue
Of summer's thorns and roses,
Its rosemary and rue,
Whose ashes will be memories
Of golden garden days and blue
To bring me back the trailing glory
Of happiness and love and you.

ILA EARLE FOWLER

STILL COVE

Jack-pine and scrub oak and the claret spires,

High huckleberry, huddled by a pond;

Sweet water, burning with reflected fires,

Black duck, landing; and, two roads beyond

Salt and sand and wading birds imaged in the blue

Wind spiced with bayberry, every twig empearled;

Shadow of a gull's wing, keening as it flew,

This is peace and wonder, in a private world

Here, I said I'd come with you; here you said, we'd be

Long before the leaves turned; but they turned too soon,

I have come without you, troubled by the sea

Stabbed by lancing sunlight, tortured by the moon.

FAITH BALDWIN

THE WALK, Thanksgiving Afternoon

On the edge of day
I come down from the pond.
Far-away leaves—

burn a witch-fire blue,
there's a rising chill
and the early dark...
and a wide field still
to be gotten through...
something small and furry
moves in the night...
but the yellow spark
of our kitchen light
streams out beyond....

and I hurry, hurry
from things that scurry...
from those who stray...
toward the safe home eaves,
and the fire, and you.

FLORENCE JACOBS

WINTER SUNSHINE

You are the sunshine
In my heart,
The radiant sunshine
Of autumn fields

Which I drink in
   As our visions store
   The golden blooms against
   The winter's yield

You are my magic
   Goldenrod,
   And the path of my day
   Is lined by you
With sunshine whenever
   you come to me,
   And the night is a crystal
   Of silvered dew.

H. CLARK BROWN

After a Storm

YOU WALK UNDER THE ICE TREES.
THEY SWAY, AND CRACKLE,
AND ARCH THEMSELVES SPLENDIDLY
TO DECK YOUR GOING.
THE WHITE SUN FLIPS THEM INTO COLOUR
BEFORE YOU.
THEY ARE BLUE,
AND MAUVE,
AND EMERALD.
THEY ARE AMBER,
AND JADE,
AND SARDONYX.
THEY ARE SILVER FRETTED TO FLAME
AND STARTLED TO STILLNESS,
BUNCHED, SPLINTERED, IRIDESCENT.
YOU WALK UNDER THE ICE TREES
AND THE BRIGHT SNOW CREAKS
                    AS YOU STEP UPON IT.
MY DOGS LEAP ABOUT YOU,
AND THEIR BARKING STRIKES UPON THE AIR
LIKE SHARP HAMMER-STROKES ON METAL.
YOU WALK UNDER THE ICE TREES
BUT YOU ARE MORE DAZZLING
                    THAN THE ICE FLOWERS,
AND THE DOGS' BARKING
IS NOT SO LOUD TO ME AS YOUR QUIETNESS.

YOU WALK UNDER THE ICE TREES
AT TEN O'CLOCK IN THE MORNING.
Amy Lowell